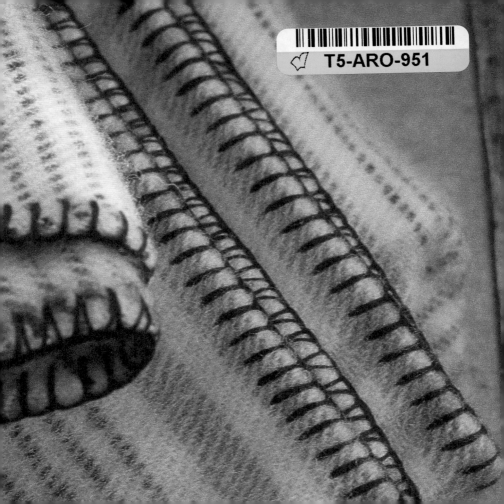

essence of WOOL

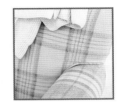

Hilary Mandleberg

e s s e n c e   o f   WOOL

RYLAND
PETERS
& SMALL

London   New York

Designer Luis Peral-Aranda
Senior Editor Sophie Bevan
Editorial Assistant Miriam Hyslop
Location Research Manager Kate Brunt
Production Gavin Bradshaw
Art Director Gabriella Le Grazie
Publishing Director Alison Starling

First published in the United Kingdom in 2001
by Ryland Peters & Small
Kirkman House, 12–14 Whitfield Street,
London W1T 2RP
www.rylandpeters.com

10 9 8 7 6 5 4 3 2 1

Text, design and photographs
© Ryland Peters & Small 2001

Jacket picture credits:
Front flap, front inset, back flap and back main image by
James Merrell
Spine and front main image by Andrew Wood

Printed and bound in China

ISBN 1 84172 190 5

A CIP record for this book is available from the British Library.

contents

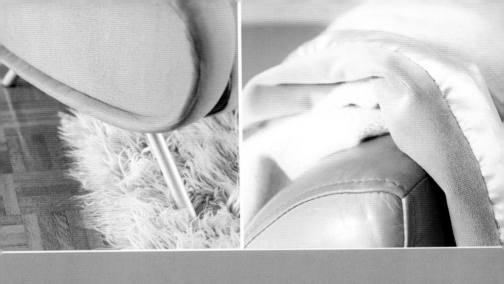

natural

Wool can be gossamer fine, coarse and nubbly, and everything between. Wear it, put it on your floors or furniture. No matter where it goes, wool is truly wonderful.

Wool comes mainly from the fleece of domesticated sheep and has been used to make our clothing and furnishings for as many as twenty-five thousand years. Prehistoric peoples clothed themselves in sheepskins and by about 3000 BC Sumerian men were depicted

SHEAR DELIGHT

wearing what appear to be jaunty woven woollen skirts. In the Bible we read of the white wool of Hebron that was traded in the markets of Damascus. And, since the Romans introduced sheep shearing, wool's quality and the range available to us has continued to improve.

Retro chic brought with it the return to favour of the natural shaggy wool rugs of the 1960s.

Wool can be processed in two ways. In the worsted system, uniform lengths of fairly fine fibres are used. These are combed and formed into strands for spinning into smooth fabrics. In the woollen system, fibres of mixed lengths are carded, then spun into a bulky, thick yarn. The finest wool is

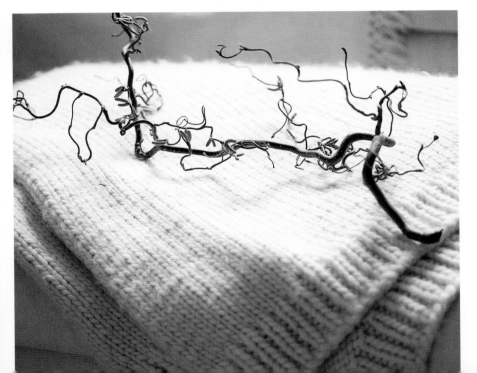

used for the finest of fabrics, while coarse wool often ends up as rugs, carpets and upholstery. Whichever you choose, see how wool appeals to the senses. Whether you opt for cuddly sheepskin, an elegant woven scarf, a chunky hand-knit or a rough goatskin laid in front of a blazing fire, there's no doubt that wool will bring you closer to nature. In your home, combine it with leather, linen, wood or stone, for a great sensual effect.

textures & colour

People have been knitting for many centuries, but its origins are a bit obscure. We do know, however, that by the seventeenth century, it was a very popular pastime for ladies. The appeal of knitted fabrics never fades. The contemporary Italian fashion company,

KNIT ONE, PURL ONE

Missoni, has made colourful, machine-made knits in fine yarns one of its trademarks. But hand-knitting is for everyone. It's satisfying, soothing and it's creative, and when you've finished, you've got something unique to wear. So pick up your needles and get going.

Wool's beautiful colours and textures serve as a great antidote to the harsh sensory effects of the modern world. Originally we dyed wool using natural plant and animal dyes – woad resulted in blues; lichens in mauves; and a certain mollusc gave the famous Tyrian purple of antiquity. Alexander the Great's father was buried in woollen clothes dyed this colour. Wool dyes very well. The dye bonds right inside the fibre. And dyes today resist fading too.

FLOATING ON AIR

Wool from sheep is only one of many possibilities. There are featherlight, yet surprisingly cosy wools that are produced by other animals. Alpaca and vicuña come from animals related to the llama; cashmere and pashm are the soft, luxurious wools of animals from Kashmir and Tibet; and angora is the long hair of Angora goats or rabbits. These are all luxury fabrics – much rarer and less hard-wearing than sheep's wool. Indulgent, but oh, so divine!

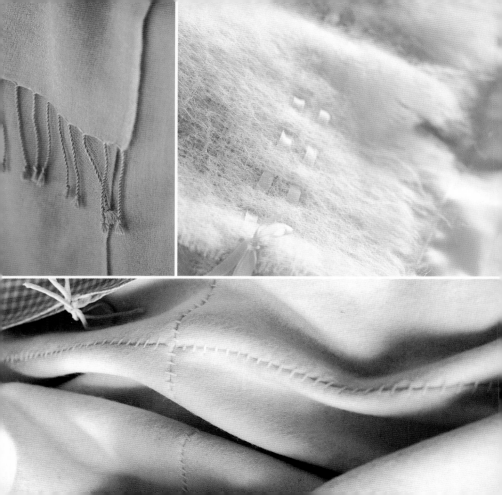

Today's interior designers are looking
back to past traditions. Both Irish and
Scottish tweeds, previously hand-dyed
and woven into shawls and blankets,

now grace the world's chic chairs and sofas, while smart rugs and carpets in Modernist designs and bold colours add softness underfoot to cold hard floors.

comfort

Wool is the ultimate when it comes to comfort. Unlike synthetics, which can absorb only about two per cent of their own weight in moisture before they start to feel damp, wool can cope with as much as thirty per cent. And because it disperses water from the skin, wool

COVER-UP

helps keep your temperature steady. Bedouin wear wool for comfort in a harsh climate that can burn by day and freeze at night. And wool gently moulds to your body, then springs back into shape. Comfort like this is just what's needed for your hectic lifestyle.

Flat-weave bright woollen rugs, soft wool blankets, tweedy throws and a pair of antlers – that's the (pioneering) spirit.

Navajo Indians wrapped up in brightly coloured blankets, while the Coast Salish wove their white blankets from the hair of a tame white dog. A modern handwoven blanket, lovingly edged in blanket stitch, is a classic too.

In the pampered, developed world, wool has moved from being a basic necessity of life - among the fabrics Colonial America imported from the mother country was the aptly named tough woollen cloth, 'fearnought' - to being a psychological comfort. Woollen

SECURITY BLANKET

blankets and sumptuous pashminas strewn across the bed not only look stylish and keep you warm, they make you feel good. Wool means a deeper sleep, too. Trials of lightweight wool cot sheets report better sleeping patterns for babies. How comforting!

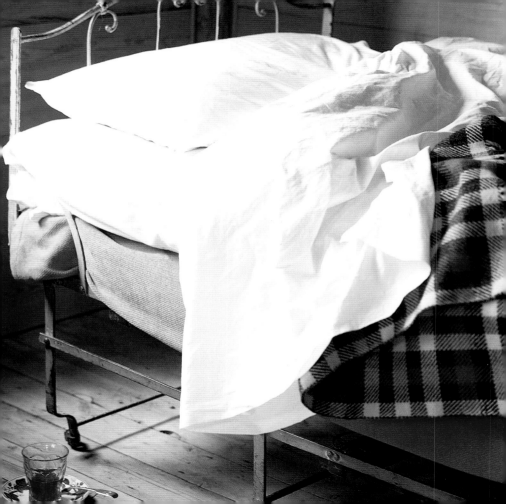

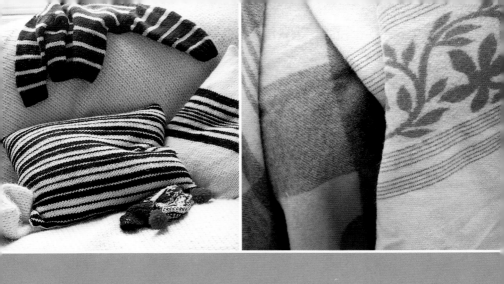

warmth

Wool of every type is just about the cosiest fabric to wrap yourself up in on a chilly winter's day. A soft, fluffy sheepskin, a pair of handknitted Fair Isle gloves or a herringbone-weave tweed scarf will keep out the harshest of winds. A variation on wool knits with

WOOLLY WARMERS

superb insulating properties is felt. It is made by applying pressure to hot, wet wool so that the fibres interlock. Felt isn't just warm, it also keeps out the wet. In Central Asia, tribesmen use felt for clothing, saddle covers, blankets and for their traditional tents, or yurts.

In period homes, antique Oriental woollen rugs on polished parquet floors add the traditional touch of warmth. For a fresh yet still cosy take on the past, look to Scandinavia. Elegant furniture painted grey, white or pale blue typified Swedish style in the eighteenth century. Warm things up a bit with soft feather pillows and a wealth of vintage wool blankets in gently faded colours, and you have a young look that is snug but still rather classic.

Warmth is something we feel on a psychological level as much as we do a physical one, and what better way to achieve that sense of wellbeing than to surround yourself with nature's handiwork? Man-made materials and striking colours all have their place in

BACK TO NATURE

our modern world, but for spiritual warmth, we can go back to our roots. For you urban rustics, a shorn sheep-skin rug laid on the floor, furniture covered in soft, forgiving wool and a knitted woollen garment on your back can't fail to work their eternal magic.

warmth

elegance

Wool has moved on a long way from the sheepskins and woven cloaks of the past. Now it can be found in the top fashion collections - black-and-white tweed dresses from Jean-Paul Gaultier, a bouclé coat by Vivienne Westwood. Finishes that control shrinkage, fresh

FASHION STATEMENT

new colour palettes, the innovative combination of wool with lycra, silk, metallic threads and other fibres - all ensure wool's lasting fashion appeal. From a classic nineteenth-century wool paisley shawl to a wool patchwork skirt by Anna Sui - it's a style must-have.

Wool and interiors are just a marriage
made in heaven. Wool shrugs off dirt;
it is strong, resilient and looks good
for years. It is ideal for luxurious yet
practical rugs and snuggle-up-to sofas.

From the fashions of the catwalk to the rooms of your house – wherever you want elegance, there you'll find wool. Interior haute couture has truly arrived. The latest wool fabrics for the home come in so many guises, you're bound to find one that will set your

BEDDED BLISS

imagination on fire. There are crisp, hard twists and tufts for floors and sofas that contrast with light-as-down knits and meshes for your throws and cushion covers. Or choose soft, blurry tweeds, flannels or twills that today's cutting-edge designers turn into table

elegance

covers, drapes and upholstery. Non-woven wools, such as felts, bring the industrial aesthetic into high-fashion interiors and special-effect yarns add refinement. This is elegance at its best.

credits

Architects and designers featured in this book and wool suppliers

Key: **a**=above, **b**=below, **l**=left, **r**=right, **t**=telephone, **f**=fax, **ph**=photographer

B. Davis
t. 001 607 264 3673
Interior design; antique hand-dyed
linen, wool, silk textiles by yard, soft
furnishings and clothing to order.
Pages 22-23, 44-45

Charlotte Crosland
Wingrave Crosland Interiors
t. 020 8960 9442
Pages 54-55

De Le Cuona Textile and Home
Collection
9-10 Osbourne Mews
Windsor SL4 3DE
e. bernie@softech.co.uk
w. www.delecuona.co.uk
Pages 11, 16-17, 47

Designers Guild
267-271 Kings Road
London SW3 5EN
t. 020 7243 7300
Pages 7 I, 12-13

Habitat UK Ltd
196 Tottenham Court Road
London W1P 9LD
t. 0645 334433 for branches.
www.habitat.co.uk

Heal's
196 Tottenham Court Road
London W1P 9LD
t. 020 7636 1666 for branches.
www.heals.co.uk

Melin Tregwynt
Melin Tregwynt Mill
Castlemorris
Haverfordwest

Pembs SA62 5UX
t. 01348 891225 for stockists
t. 01348 891644 for mail order

MODÉNATURE
Créations Henry Becq
3, rue Jacob et 59, rue de Seine
75006 Paris, France
Page 14

Natural Flooring Direct
P.O. Box 8104
London SE16 4ZA
t. 0800 454721

Johnson Naylor
13 Britton Street
London EC1M 5SX
t. 020 7490 8885
f. 020 7490 0038
Page 61

OKA Direct
A unique collection of mail order
furniture and accessories for the
home including rattan, painted
furniture, leather and horn.
For a catalogue call 0870 160 6002
www.okadirect.com
Page 60

Roger Oates Design
Shop & Showroom:
1 Munro Terrace, Cheyne Walk
London SW10 0DL
Studio Shop:
The Long Barn
Eastnor, Ledbury
Herefordshire HR8 1EL
Rugs and runners mail order
catalogue:
t. 01531 631 611
Pages 36-37, 54, 55

The Scotch House
165 Regent Street
London W1B 4PH
t. 020 7734 4060

Selfridges & Co.
400 Oxford Street
London W1A 1AB
t. 020 7629 1234
www.selfridges.co.uk

Sequana
64 Avenue de la Motte
Picquet
75015 Paris, France
t. 00 33 1 45 66 58 40
f. 00 33 1 45 67 99 81
Pages 26, 27, 30, 35, 48-49, 50

Sixty 6
66 Marylebone High Street
London W1M 3AH
t. 020 7224 6066
Vintage furniture, clothes and
accessories.
Pages 28, 29

Stephen Slan, AIA
Variations in Architecture Inc.
2156 Hollyridge Drive
Los Angeles
California 90068, USA
t. 001 323 467 4455
f. 001 323 467 6655
Pages 1, 56-57

Wool Classics
41 Ledbury Road
London W11 2AA
t. 020 7792 8277

picture credits

Endpapers ph Andrew Wood

1 ph James Merrell; **2 ph** Andrew Wood/Media executive's house in Los Angeles, Architect: Stephen Slan; Builder: Ken Duran, Furnishings: Russell Simpson, Original Architect: Carl Maston c. 1945; **3 ph** Tom Leighton; **4-5 ph** Sandra Lane; **6 ph** Andrew Wood; **7 l ph** Andrew Wood/Neil Bingham's house in Blackheath, London, chair courtesy of Designer's Guild; **7 r ph** Polly Wreford/Glenn Carwithen & Sue Miller's house in London; **8 ph** Polly Wreford/Mary Foley's house in Connecticut; **11 ph** Andrew Wood/Bernie de le Cuona's house in Windsor; **12-13 ph** Andrew Wood/Neil Bingham's house in Blackheath, London, chair courtesy of Designer's Guild; **14 ph** David Montgomery/Designer of Modénature Henry Becq's apartment in Paris; **15 ph** James Merrell; **16-17 ph** Andrew Wood/Bernie de le Cuona's house in Windsor; **18 & 19 l ph** Sandra Lane; **19 r ph** David Montgomery; **20 ph** James Merrell; **22-23 ph** James Merrell/Barbara Davis' house in upstate New York; **24-25 al & b ph** James Merrell; **25 ar ph** Sandra Lane; **26 & 27 ph** Andrew Wood/Mary Shaw's Sequana apartment in Paris; **28 & 29 ph** Andrew Wood/Jane Collins of Sixty 6 in Marylebone High Street, home in central London; **30 ph** Andrew Wood/Mary Shaw's Sequana apartment in Paris; **31 l ph** Andrew Wood; **31 r & 32 ph** Tom Leighton; **34 ph** Simon Upton/Susan & Jerry Lauren's Connecticut home; **35 ph** Andrew Wood/Mary Shaw's Sequana apartment in Paris; **36-37 main and inset ph** Andrew Wood/Roger Oates & Fay Morgan's house in Eastnor; **38 ph** James Merrell/Gabriele Sanders' apartment in New York; **40 ph** Tom Leighton/Mr. Hone's 17th Century hutt in Shropshire; **41 l & r ph** James Merrell; **43 ph** James Merrell; **44-45 ph** James Merrell/Barbara Davis' house in upstate New York; **47 ph** Andrew Wood/Bernie de le Cuona's house in Windsor; **48-49 & 50 ph** Andrew Wood/Mary Shaw's Sequana apartment in Paris; **51 l & r & 52 ph** James Merrell; **54-55 ph** Andrew Wood/Charlotte Crosland's house in London; **56-57 ph** Andrew Wood/Media executive's house in Los Angeles, Architect: Stephen Slan; Builder: Ken Duran, Furnishings: Russell Simpson, Original Architect: Carl Maston c. 1945; **58 ph** James Merrell/Gabriele Sanders' apartment in New York; **60 ph** David Montgomery/Annabel Astor's house in London is full of furniture and accessories designed exclusively for her OKA Direct Mail order catalogue; **61 ph** Andrew Wood/Roger & Suzy Black's apartment in London designed by Johnson Naylor.

The author and publisher would also like to thank all those whose homes or work are featured in this book.

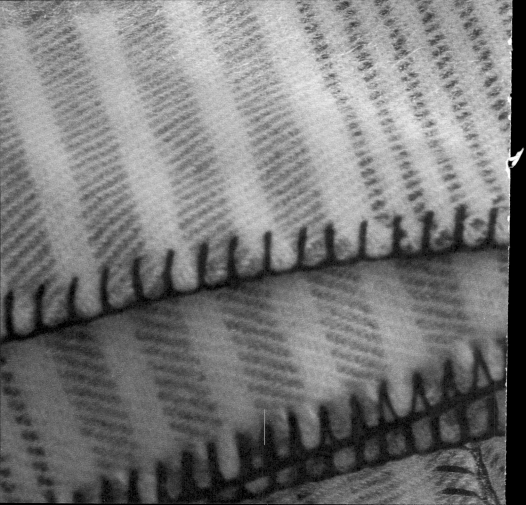